Summa

C000103079

Power of Now

A Guide to Spiritual Enlightenment by
Eckhart Tolle

Summareads Media

Get 2 summary books that we're

giving away for FREE. Visit:

www.summareads.com

allowed unless with written permission from the publisher. All rights reserved.

The information provided herein is stated to be truthful and consistent, in that any liability, in terms of inattention or otherwise, by any usage or abuse of any policies, processes, or directions contained within is the solitary and utter responsibility of the recipient reader. Under no circumstances will any legal responsibility or blame be held against the publisher for any reparation, damages, or monetary loss due to the information herein, either directly or indirectly.

Respective authors own all copyrights not held by the publisher.

The information herein is offered for informational purposes solely, and is universal as so. The presentation of the information is without contract or any type of guarantee assurance.

The trademarks that are used are without any consent, and the publication of the trademark is without permission or backing by the trademark owner. All trademarks and brands within this book are for clarifying purposes only and are owned by the owners themselves, not affiliated with this document.

Table of Contents

INTRODUCTION - Notes from SummaReads Media Team

In this book, Tolle offers a unique perspective created with a combination of modern and ancient approaches to spirituality. He takes the traditionally personified view of Christ and transforms it into an omnipresent, eternal source of energy that he believes anyone can and should tap into.

This book has the potential to be a great resource for anyone who is seeking new perspectives on physical and spiritual well-being. It will be even more beneficial to you if you are also seeking to develop a stronger relationship with Christ. At the same time, you can tap into the numerous potential advantages of modern meditative practices and easily incorporate them into your daily life.

With his unique ideas, Tolle will show you how to leave the past behind you and abandon your fears for the future. In their place, he will help you encourage a strong sense of inner peace and appreciation for the current moment.

POWER PRINCIPLES

-   Your Being is the essence of your true self—the part of you that lives on after your body dies. Connecting with your being will help you achieve enlightenment.

-   View the present moment objectively. Dwelling on situations in an emotional way only brings pain.

-   Time and problems are illusions. By living in the Now, you will learn to accept things as they are and either act to change or embrace the current situation.

-   Be constantly aware of your emotions. They signal that action should be taken or a change in perspective is needed.

-   By connecting with your Being, you will connect with the Source of all things: Christ. Everything in existence is an eternal part of this Source.

- Do not judge or ignore your body. By being aware of your body—both inner (spiritual) and outer (physical)—you connect to your Being.

- There are many portals to the source. The Now is one of the most important.

- Relationships do not bring salvation, but they are great opportunities for us to conquer unconsciousness. By doing this, we connect deeper with our Being and in turn, with God.

- Happiness depends on circumstances being met. Alternatively, inner peace has no such conditions. It can be found even in terrible situations.

- Let your Being drive your actions, not your emotions. Feelings are signals for change, but they should not rule our lives.

SUPER SUMMARY

CHAPTER 1 - The Definitions of Being

People who are seeking something—happiness, wealth, enlightenment, often fail to look within themselves. Tolle believes that the ultimate enlightenment can be found within the radiant joy of **Being**. It is not an unattainable, extraordinary accomplishment; it is your natural state of oneness. In fact, Tolle quotes The Buddha's simplistic definition of enlightenment: "the end of suffering".

For the purposes of this book, "Being" is defined as the eternal 'One Life' beyond the mundane—the indestructible essence of every being. It is not something that can be understood, only felt in your calmest states. While readers may be inclined to simply label this as "God", Tolle believes that this term is severely over-used. As such, it has lost true meaning and become confined to a closed concept with set representations. Alternatively, Being is a more open concept.

The greatest obstacle toward this enlightened awareness is our own inner chatter. We often equate identity and Being with thinking. This concept only enhances our separateness from our true selves. To truly understand our Being is to know that we are connected to everything around us. We are not our minds, and our minds should not be using us. We should be using them as an extension of our true selves. We should be able to have such control of our minds that we can 'unplug' ourselves from incessant thoughts whenever we want.

Most human minds are in a constant state of inner dialogue. The first step in quieting these voices is to take the time to listen to them. Pay attention to your repetitive thought patterns. As you observe, do your best to remain impartial, as if you are an observer of the inner workings of your mind rather than an active participant. This will help you enter a new phase of consciousness.

In-between your thoughts, there are gaps—often called 'the mind of no mind'. As you work to gain your sense of inner peace, these gaps will become larger. The joy you feel in this state is the subtle emanation of Being. This does not mean you are in a trance-like or unconscious state. Rather, you are more aware—more conscious.

Another way to quiet your inner chatter is to redirect your attention. Practice becoming conscious of the present moment alone. This will create a similar gap in your stream of consciousness, allowing you to reach that ideal state more easily. You will know that you are succeeding by the increasing sense of peace you feel within.

You may wonder if quelling your thoughts will do more harm than good. Tolle believes this is not the case. He says that the majority of people's thinking is not only repetitive and unconstructive, it is also often negative or harmful.

Part of the reason so many people feel the need to think so heavily is that they identify themselves by their thoughts. For the purposes of this book Tolle calls this our "ego"; it is our false sense of self perpetuated by our thoughts.

To our ego selves, the past and future are the only relevant things. The present does not truly exist. When the ego self looks at the present, it is always through the lens of the past or future—never as it truly is.

Some may be concerned that the approach Tolle is proposing will inhibit their analytical and discriminatory abilities. They feel that their ability to think is what places them superior to other living creatures. Tolle believes that this type of thought is simply a stage in evolution. It is our job to progress to the next stage of consciousness—with the awareness that thinking and consciousness are not synonymous. The next stage of awareness eliminates involuntary internal dialogue. The state of mental peace is the key to tapping into our natural creative abilities.

For the purposes of this book, "thought" also includes emotions. They are the connection between your mind and body. Unconscious emotional patterns can be even more dangerous than involuntary thoughts; they should be dealt with using the same strategies.

If, while observing yourself, you notice a conflict between your thoughts and your body (example: your mind says "no" to an impulse while your body says "yes"), your emotions will be the key to your true state of mind at the time.

Tolle believes that all negative emotions are a variation of one—your loss of awareness of who you are. The closest label he can fit to this concept is "**pain**". The mind is constantly fighting to remove that emotional pain. Unfortunately, this can never be achieved while you continue to view your thoughts and emotions as your identity.

Alternatively, positive thoughts—love, peace, and joy—are interconnected with your state of Being. Typical people often only experience the deeper connection to this in brief spurts—when they are rendered speechless in a positive way. Pleasure is not included in this state because it often comes from something outside of yourself, and will inevitably bring you pain.

It is also important to be aware of cravings. These are the mind's attempts to seek fulfillment outside of itself. Your efforts to become enlightened should not be a craving, but rather a state of living with present awareness.

CHAPTER 2 - The Trouble With Pain

Tolle believes that the majority of human pain is unnecessary and self-created. It is usually caused by a person's inability or unwillingness to **accept what is**. The degree of intensity depends on the level of resistance to the present moment. This is because the unenlightened mind often perceives timeless concepts as threatening.

Too many people let the concept of time itself take over their lives. They focus too heavily on the past or future while ignoring the precious nature of the present moment. As such, they continue to add to their pain by rejecting joy. The key to preventing time from taking over your life is to make the present moment your priority.

It is also important not to label the present moment. It should simply be accepted as it is. Accept, then act; work with the current situation, rather than resisting it.

Do not dwell on the past; that is often the source of our pain. Our bodies have been flooded by past suffering that, if left unchecked, will inhibit our joy. Sometimes, we feel this pain only in certain situations that remind us—consciously or unconsciously—of our past. Other times, it becomes an overlay for our entire existence.

This pain manifests in different ways for different people and may also change as we age. Depression, abuse, violence, and mental illness can be triggered by these past pains. Even behavior problems in children can be a result of this harbored toxic energy.

These emotional issues can happen suddenly and cause unpleasant surprises for those around you. This is why it is especially important to pay attention to your own emotional reactions before they take over. You may be able to save yourself and others from a world of hurt.

Your pain-body wants to survive, just like any living being on the planet. It feeds off the attention you give it—the moments that you allow it to take over your life. It feeds off those who let it take over their understanding of who they are until they are their own pain. Then, these people either become perpetrators who cause pain, or victims who constantly find ways to live in pain. This is where your mental state comes in. If you can pay conscious attention to your thought patterns, you may be able to stop these toxic cycles from taking hold. Observe it objectively, just like you do with your other thoughts and emotions. Do not attempt to fight it, but instead, work to accept what is happening in the present. Then, it will lose its power over you.

It is especially important to know who you are without your thoughts and without your pain. Sometimes, people tend to hold on to their suffering because they are afraid of who they might be without it.

Tolle believes that we do not need fear to avoid unnecessary danger—that the necessity of fear in our survival is a myth. Fear itself is usually triggered by emotion about things that aren't currently happening.

All we need to survive is **common sense**. This is one of the few times where remembering the trials of our past can be helpful. These experiences will help us determine how to approach the present.

Fear is another main trigger for conflict. We often fear being wrong or otherwise disillusioned about our self-identity. This is why it is so important to approach your thoughts and emotions in an objective way, rather than attaching yourself to them.

Another aspect of emotional pain is rooted in our common quest for wholeness. This can be either conscious or unconscious, but there is a bit of it in all of us. Unconsciously, it is typically felt as an intense craving for something, such as love, money, or success. The problem is, even when people attain the things they think they need, that hole within them is still there. This is why it is important not to let your ego run your life, or you will forever be identifying yourself by what you have rather than who you are.

CHAPTER 3 - The Truth About Suffering

Some people think that you first need to seek to understand the inner workings of your mind before you can achieve full consciousness and enlightenment. Tolle believes that this is absolutely untrue. In fact, by now, you have already learned the first key to enlightenment: that your thoughts are not your identity, and treating it as such—while common—will only pull you further away from your true sense of Being. Once you know this basic dysfunction, there is no need to explore its various facets.

A healthy mind can be a wonderful tool. When you work to be present within the moment, you can accept your mind for what it is, rather than letting it tangle itself within your life and sense of identity. The key to doing this is to end the illusion of time. Remove your endless occupation with past and future and allow the **present moment** to envelop you.

Many people feel the opposite about time. They feel that time is very precious and should be used wisely rather than wasted. Many readers may ask what is so bad about acknowledging time, since our past helped us become who we are and our future goals determine our present actions. However, Tolle believes that this is a harmful perspective. **Time is an illusion**. The past and future are nowhere near as precious as the present. This is because, to Tolle, the present is all there is. Trying to over-analyze the illusion of time is to surrender yourself to the very superficial mind you've been working to separate from your true self.

One way that typical people experience full immersion in the present is through death-defying activities such as rock climbing, racing, etc. But you do not need these kinds of experiences to feel the present moment. You can do it right now. Simply withdraw your attention from the past and future when that attention is not in immediate need. Then, turn your attention to experiencing the present moment without judgement.

The power of fully experiencing the present moment is often addressed in various religions and philosophies. There is certainly a place for knowledge and efforts to understand, but many people still neglect this power: the power to simply be.

Once you have learned to live in the moment at will, then you can slowly bring back your ability to use the past and future for practical purposes. You can learn from your past, set goals for the future, and even predict what may happen using analytical computations. As you work through these things, never lose your grip on the present, since any action your take based on your analysis will be implemented now.

Be careful to keep your perception of time as a practical, objective understanding. Do not allow it to take over your life or decisions in that you only dwell on the past, or you only make decisions with thought of the future. Do not allow yourself to become so preoccupied with where you have been or where you are going, that you forget to appreciate where you are.

People tend to harbor this belief that they should look toward the future because it will always be better than the present. In reality, the future is often a replica of the past in many ways. Real change can only happen if you bring your focus into the power of the present.

Many believe that suffering is caused by situations and/or people. Alternatively, Tolle believes that all negativity is caused by an inability to live in the present: either dwelling on the past or worrying about the future. You can only be free of these worries if you free yourself from them by living in the present.

Some may feel reluctant to be aware of their present because they view it to be unhappy or unpleasant. In reality, this is still bound by the restrictions of time. Unhappiness about our lives is typically caused by issues with the past and/or resistance to the present. Work to become fully aware of your current situation as it is at this very moment. Then, you may find that you are not suffering as much as you perceive. There is a difference between your life situation and your life—the fact that you are alive right now. Take a moment to accept things as they are and simply experience them objectively, rather than judging them.

Some may feel that these efforts to be present are pointless, since they will not solve any of our problems. In fact, Tolle believes that problems themselves are illusions. Instead, everything that happens to us should be viewed as a situation— either something that we can actively change, or something that should be accepted as an aspect of the present. Do not make your situations into problems by dwelling on them with no intention or ability to solve them at this point in time.

As an example, think of a true emergency. In these situations, your mind does not have time to create a problem out of what it is experiencing. Instead, it simply assesses the situation objectively, and you take action.

If you find yourself resistant to this idea, remember: we often reject things that threaten our perception of ourselves. We define ourselves by our suffering. When this identity is threatened, we reject it rather than allowing ourselves to be free. In reality, this approach to life is the only way that we can progress into the next stage of our evolution.

One easy way to assess whether you are living in the moment is to look for joy. If you cannot find the joy in what you are currently doing, you are allowing yourself to become burdened by time. **If you cannot change what you are doing, change how you are doing it.** Become less concerned with the future results of your actions and instead, focus on the action itself. This will help it to become an effort of joy, rather than one of suffering. The moment your attention turns back to the Now, you connect with the essence of Being, and reach a state of peace.

You may wonder if finally achieving this state of wholeness and contentment will harm your future achievements. Tolle says that we can most certainly continue to strive for our goals, and we should not lose our motivation to do so. The difference will be in our approach. We will no longer be relying on acquired things to make us happy. Instead, you will be achieving just for achievement's sake. At this point, you will understand that nothing of true value can be threatened, and you can surrender yourself to the joy of your present experience.

CHAPTER 4 - The Problems of the Past

You may wonder: even if you do accept that time is an illusion, how will this help when you live in a world completely dominated by time? The answer is simple: as your perspective changes, so will your experience. Continue to work to shift your consciousness toward the present moment. Then, the moments when you must perceive time for practicality's sake, your attitude toward the situation will improve and you will be able to return more easily to your state of peace.

The key to this, as mentioned before, is to adjust your consciousness. People often use unconsciousness as an escape from their current situation. When faced with a challenge, they move further and further away from their present. Alternatively, you should do the opposite; face your challenges head-on, then choose—**action or acceptance**. This is why you must practice living in the Now with simple situations. This will help make it easier for you when situations are more complicated.

People who are preoccupied with time are always seeking something. This causes persistent anxiety and tension. This is why it is so important to facilitate your enlightenment by remaining conscious of these negative thoughts and feelings within yourself. When you become aware of them, you take away their power. Frequently ask yourself: Am I at ease at this moment? What am I feeling right now? Is there any area of my body that feels tense? Why?

Be especially aware of feelings of resentment. Tune into that emotion and observe your other thoughts and physical reactions in response to it. This will help you to accept the underlying situation as it is and prevent toxic emotions from poisoning your well-being. If necessary, it will also help you choose an action to change the situation. Remember: situations just are. They are only made good or bad by our own **perspectives**.

To be clear, this does not mean that negative feelings, such as resentment, should be rejected. Instead, they act as a signal that your perspective needs to be adjusted and/or that action needs to be taken. Tolle encourages you to focus on more positive emotions because joy is a conscious choice that will improve your well-being. The more you indulge your more positive emotions, the fewer negative emotions you will feel.

Complaint is a strong indicator of unconscious negativity. Pay particular attention to your complaints—both mental and verbal. This is a clear sign that either you have chosen not to change or remove yourself from your current situation, or you have chosen not to accept the present moment as it is. You should not be waiting for your life to change. You should be changing it yourself through action or acceptance.

When you do take action, do not do it from a negative place. Instead, try to do it **objectively**— viewing what is required rather than allowing your negative feelings to overtake you. Then, **let the**

past go. Remember: The past and future should only be addressed when they are absolutely relevant to the present moment.

Some may feel that a focus on the future is important—that it helps give our lives purpose. While it is certainly helpful to have future goals in perspective, do not let it take away from your experience in the present moment.

Tolle believes that your life's journey has both an inner and outer purpose. The outer is to arrive at your goal or destination. The inner journey only involves the step you are taking right now. In the grand scheme of things, he believes that whether you succeed or not in your outer journey will not matter. Ultimately, all that will matter is the fulfillment of your inner purpose. The outer purpose will end; it is impermanent. The inner purpose is eternal.

Some may wonder about the efficacy of analyzing your past. In truth, anything about your past that you will need to address will be brought up in your future challenges. So, there is no need to consciously analyze it beforehand. As you become more conscious in your present, you will gain the necessary insights about yourself to help you address your current challenges.

CHAPTER 5 - The Potential in the Present

It is important to remember that being present is not something you need to understand, only do. On that note, Tolle suggests an experiment: Close your eyes and say or think to yourself "What is my next thought going to be?" Then, wait for your next thought to arrive, like a predator stalking its prey.

You may find that, when you are in this state of presence, it may take time for your next clear thought to come. This is an example of what it is like to be present, and why it is not necessary to seek to understand that state. The key aspect of this state is to stay 'fully rooted' within your body. Maintaining a sense of self-awareness will keep you anchored into the present time.

Many of us experience this kind of state in brief flashes, which is something Zen masters call 'satori'. It is a brief moment of enlightenment that gives you a taste of what you could achieve. As you continue to work to develop your mental health, you will find that these moments will lengthen. That is your goal.

Being able to be completely aware of the present will help you see and appreciate the intense beauty in every moment. It will do this by helping you to connect with Being, as described in Chapter 1. Everything in existence has Being. Acknowledging this will help you to understand that you are merely a thread in the woven tapestry of existence—that your life is connected to everything else. This will help you to understand that your Being is eternal, and only its vessel changes.

The opposite of this consciousness is embodied in the harmful habits that people take on throughout their lives: through substance abuse, sex, gambling, and other addictions. People use these things to escape from the present moment. These choices could mean our downfall. Tolle believes that the only way that the human species will survive is through their transformation to the next phase of consciousness.

Utilizing silence is one great way to become present. Taking advantage of a silent moment, and becoming silent yourself, will help encourage you to live in the moment. This creates a sense of stillness within you.

For the purposes of this book, 'the presence' is defined as your mostly-unconscious connection to your divine self. 'Christ' is defined as the awakened version of this connection—your enlightened consciousness. If you like, you can think of Christ as the eternal consciousness of Jesus.

Tolle believes that the second coming of Christ is actually the transformation of the human consciousness. He thinks that the personalization of Christ is a mistake—that in truth, we should accept Christ as a master, but also a reflection of your own identity. This means that when we seek to understand our Being, we are actually seeking to understand Christ's presence within us.

Group work may also help you achieve your enlightenment. The presence of others working collectively toward a common goal may help you reach that state of 'mind of no mind'—where your Being resides. However, it is important that at least one member of the group is firmly established. This will help create an anchor that new members can cling to for guidance.

CHAPTER 6 - Connecting the Dots

Before we continue, it is important to remember not to seek to understand Being. It is something you should seek to **feel**—not to understand. This state of Being is your true self. It is free from the restrictions from the mind, body, and fear. It is free from the sin of your suffering—the pain you bring upon yourself.

Now, some may find the word 'sin' to be unpleasant—that it implies judgement or punishment. Instead, Tolle believes that you should view this word just as you view your thoughts—**objectively**, for what it is, and without the common emotional connotations. If necessary, you can also replace it for another word—so long as that word embodies the same meaning as what he means by 'sin' in this case. There is no need to condemn—only observe and learn from what you see.

Tolle also wants to clarify what he means by 'being conscious of your body'. In this case, what he means is being aware of the life force within your body. This is the beginning of your journey to peace and the reality of your Being.

One way to encourage this awareness is through a simple exercise. Begin by closing your eyes. This may not be necessary later, but it can be quite helpful when you are first beginning your practice. Then, turn your attention toward the feel of the life force within your body—beginning by focusing on one body part at a time, then expanding your awareness to your body as a whole. During this process, pay attention to what you feel. If thoughts or images come to mind, make note of those too. Before you end the exercise, take a moment to open your eyes and look around the room—all while continuing to focus primarily on your body.

Some may wonder why Tolle puts so much focus on the body here, since many religions or philosophies regard the body as a hindrance—or even harmful. Commonly, bodies are regarded as a separate entity that you must control. You may have even gotten this impression from the earlier chapters from this book. But here, Tolle clarifies that the body is an important tool to reach enlightenment. We must seek to become aware of our body and accept it for what it is in order to reach the next stage of growth.

In addition, in reference to the various religions and philosophies, Tolle asserts that all teachings are originally derived from a single source. As such, there is truly only one 'master' who just happens to manifest in various forms. One of these forms is ourselves. Since we are all connected, we are all part of that divine source power.

The key to achieving this awareness is maintaining a consistent connection with your 'inner body', as defined in earlier chapters. The more attention you give this part of yourself, the stronger it will become, and the less likely pain will be able to sink its hold into you. This is because keeping your attention on the body will help you stay anchored in the present moment.

As you go about your daily activities, you should also seek to keep this awareness. Try to maintain your consciousness of your inner body as you move, act, and interact. In other words: no matter what you do, stay rooted within yourself. This will be especially helpful when things go wrong. In fact, whenever you are faced with a challenge, the key to conquering it is to go even deeper into this root. Do not allow your mind and emotions to take hold of you. Instead, cling to this anchor, and remember who you are at the root of your Being.

Sometimes, when readers have attempted to perform these body awareness exercises, they have felt uncomfortable or even unwell. Tolle believes that this is likely residual emotion or issues that you are yet unaware of. These are moments when it is especially important to acknowledge the emotion and then accept (aka. forgive) it for what it is, just as you have done in the past with your other thoughts and emotions. Remember: emotions are always temporary, but your Being is eternal.

For the purposes of this book, you should view 'presence' as pure consciousness contained within your inner body. Your inner body is your link with the 'Unmanifested', which is the Source of true consciousness. So, in being aware of your inner body, you are tapping into the Source. In this case, you can consider it the same as the Unmanifested, because you have not yet tapped into your Being.

Some of this information may be difficult to process. Tolle believes that when you reach a certain phase of your consciousness, you will be able to recognize truth when you hear it. This will help enhance your ability to process the information that he is sharing.

In addition to the spiritual benefits, becoming more aware of your body can have physical benefits as well. Tolle believes that this regular practice can actually slow the aging process of your physical (or 'outer') body. This is because your inner body, if maintained, will remain the same and your outer body will feel more alive. For those who wonder whether there is scientific evidence to support this,

Tolle answers that if you are able to maintain this practice, you yourself will be the evidence to support this perspective.

Tolle also believes that this practice will strengthen your immune system. This is based on the belief that, when you are not present within your inner body, illnesses have a greater ability to take root— kind of a 'when the cat is away, the mice will play' concept.

There are also benefits to your psychic immune system. This will help protect you from the negative emotions of others. It will give you the ability to operate on a different level of consciousness from these low-level energies so that they will either pass by you, or not interact with you at all.

There are simple practices you can do to boost your immune system. These are especially helpful if you employ them at the first sign of any illness. Though, they can still be used after an illness has already taken hold. However, keep in mind that they should not be used as a substitute for your daily practice of consciousness.

One such exercise only takes a few moments of your time. It can be done any time you have a few minutes to spare—or ideally, right before you go to sleep and then again as soon as you awaken. The steps are included below:

- Position yourself comfortably by lying flat on your back.

- Close your eyes.

- Practice focusing your attention on different parts of your body, one at a time, for at least 15 seconds each.

- Allow your attention to flicker briefly across your entire body, from head to toe and back up again. This should take only about a minute.

- Take a moment to simply experience what you are feeling now, with your energy fully centered within your inner body. If you find your mind wandering, try not to worry. Simply turn your attention back to your body.

If at any time you are finding it difficult to do this exercise or other similar procedures to get in touch with your inner body, focusing on your breath can be a helpful start. **Conscious breathing** is a powerful meditation tool in its own right and it will be very beneficial in your practices. If you find it easier to visualize, you can also imagine yourself breathing in white light that begins to surround your entire Being. As you become more adept, bring your focus away from the images and onto the simple feeling of this exercise.

If you need to use your mind for a specific purpose, remember to tap into your inner body first. This also applies to your interactions with other people. Work to feel your inner body as you listen, instead of just listening with your mind. This will prevent your unconscious thoughts from overpowering what you are hearing. In turn, this will help you connect more deeply with others.

CHAPTER 7 - The Source and Death

If you are having some difficulty going deeper into your inner body, try using some of these tips:

- Eliminate as many external distractions as you can.

- Sit comfortably in a chair, but do not lean back. Keep the spine straight.

- If you choose a different meditative position, make sure that you are able to keep the spine straight and keep yourself alert throughout the process.

- Close your eyes.

- Start each session by consciously relaxing your body

- When you get distracted, focus on your breath.

- Most importantly: practice! Ten to fifteen minutes per session is all you really need.

Some readers may wonder if what Tolle refers to as "the Unmanifested" is the same as 'Chi'—an eastern term for universal life energy. Tolle says that they are not the same. In this case, consider Chi your inner body—while the Unmanifested is the source. Think of Chi like a moving river leading you to the still ocean of the Source. As you continue the practices already detailed in this book, it will make it easier and easier to connect with this energy.

Tolle says that when you enter the phase of dreamless sleep each night, this is you connecting directly with the source. In this case, it is unconscious but with practice, you will be able to do this consciously as well. However, it is not necessary to attempt to remain conscious while in a dreamless sleep. This act of 'lucid dreaming' may be fascinating, but according to Tolle, it is not nearly as liberating as willingly connecting with the source on a conscious level.

You can consider your inner body as a 'portal' to the Source—one of several others. The others have already been mentioned in this book previously, but for easy study, we will revisit them briefly here:

- The Now

The present moment is a key portal to the Source. You cannot be in touch with your body without being wholly in the present.

- Mind of No Mind

When you can stop your unconscious stream of thoughts, you can better channel your energy into your conscious awareness.

- Surrender

When you accept what is as it is and cease your resistance of the truth, you will become more open to the joys of the present moment.

- Silence

Pay attention to the sounds you hear. The silence from which they emerge and return is also a portal to the Source. Silence enables sound to be, just as the Source is the energy from which all things are born and to which they return.

- Space

Similar to the concepts around sound, empty space is also a portal to the source. But it will only work this way so long as you do not seek to understand it or make it into something it is not. Simply feel it and accept it for what it is, especially since it, like time, is an illusion.

You may be wondering why love is not mentioned as a portal. For the purposes of this book, consider love as a by-product of your efforts. As soon as you open a portal, you connect with love.

If the ideas of space and silence bewilder you, remember that we would not be able to recognize presence and sound without them. **Space is the source of shape and silence is the source of sound.**

Even if you have missed all of your other opportunities to access portals to the Source, your final chance remains in the moment of your physical death. This experience has been recounted by countless others when they had near-death experiences.

Tolle believes that upon death, most people turn away from the Source in fear, and fall into unconsciousness until they are once again born into another physical body and start all over again. However, if one is enlightened, they will face and accept the Source, and ascend into a state of eternal consciousness.

CHAPTER 8 - The Truth About Salvation

It is a common belief that true enlightenment can only be achieved through a loving relationship between a man and a woman. However, Tolle says that the problem with this idea is that then, we are waiting for a moment in time to save us. **In reality, salvation is in the here and now.** True happiness and salvation is living in the moment, rather than dwelling on the past or constantly seeking something that will 'make you whole'.

In terms of this book, salvation is defined as freedom from fear, suffering, and a sense of incompleteness. In truth, we find God the moment we realize that we do not need to seek God. By living in the present, we are already living with God.

Living in the Now also helps us with other areas of our lives, such as our relationships. Relationships living outside of the present moment are often rampant with discord. It may seem like you only need to eliminate or repair destructive cycles in these relationships, but in reality, this is not possible. Being 'in love' with your partner is not enough to save you from the negativity from toxic emotions like jealousy, neediness, and control.

Romantic love is often viewed as a form of salvation because it gives us those feelings of wholeness and freedom. However, in this case, those feelings are temporary. Physically, you will never be whole, because you are essentially one half of a Being—either man or woman. While we commonly seek wholeness through romantic love or sex, this will only offer the briefest of glimpses.

It is also important to recognize that true love does not have a negative aspect. It is not possible to truly love your partner one moment and then attack them in one way or another in the next. When you feel like your partner is behaving in a way that fails to meet your needs, the real problem is that you are letting your ego take over your true self. This situation is only a shallow shadow of love—addiction and need disguised as the true state. You are projecting your painful feelings outward.

Other forms of addiction work this way as well. They are simply another way for you to hide from your pain, rather than dealing with it. They are another way for you to attempt escape from the salvation of the present. But it is important to remember that avoidance is not the answer.

The key to facing your present and turning your shallow relationships into true ones is to abide by the guidelines listed in this book. By living in the moment, you will bring substance to your life and live as your true self.

For the purposes of this book, God is defined as that one life that connects all of our lives. Love is defined as feeling that presence whole-heartedly— both within yourself and others. Therefore, all love is actually a love of God.

Love is not selective, judgemental, or exclusive. Only the degree of intensity with which you feel it is different. True communication between you and those you love is actually communion—a realization of that oneness.

These issues that people have with their relationships, and the misidentification of love, are very common. And while this is certainly a terrible realization, it can also be viewed as an opportunity. This is the perfect time for you to practice your mindfulness and focus on the present. Once you can fully accept the facts within these situations, you can finally realize even more opportunity for spiritual growth. Remember: this is not about changing who you are. Instead, it is about not allowing surface-level aspects of your life to define you. It is about knowing and accepting your true Being.

Whenever there is strife in your relationships, be glad. This is the perfect opportunity for unconscious issues to come to light. This is the perfect time for you to understand that you will not find salvation through your relationship, which will help you to accept your partner as they are, instead of expecting them to complete you.

It is also important to remember that it is not your job to enlighten your partner. You can only enlighten yourself. Taking on the role of mentor when it has not been asked for will only bring out your ego. Instead, you must relinquish all judgement. This does not mean that you do not recognize the dysfunction, only that you are allowing it to be and adjusting your own reaction. By being an example of true enlightenment, you will be the greatest catalyst for the transformation of those around you.

True enlightenment is characterized by an emanation of joy and acceptance for all beings as well as being fully present in the moment. This or the lack of it will be especially obvious when things go wrong, as discussed in earlier chapters about personal development.

Tolle believes that while the obstacles to enlightenment are the same for both men and women, the emphasis on each is different. Typically, it is easier for a woman to become enlightened, because it is easier for them to feel their inner body. In many ancient texts, women were viewed as a direct line to the Source—

embodiments of the Unmanifested. It was only later, when society became male-dominated, that the divine was labeled as male. This does not mean that the author thinks we should revert to a feminine divinity model, but only that we should acknowledge the primary difference between male and female: men are often anchored within their mind—their thoughts are their primary obstacle—while women are more prone to visits to their inner selves.

Alternatively, pain is much more of an obstacle for women. Those who still live in a state of unconsciousness not only suffer from their own pain, but also from the collective pain of those around them. The majority of this pain may lie dormant most of the time, but often awakens around the time of a woman's menstrual flow. The key to overcoming this is to remember that the pain that you feel is not your identity. You must identify your true self, outside of this pain. When your menstrual flow nears, be especially vigilant not to let your pain take over. It is also helpful to make sure your romantic partner understands this about you. They should know that when your pain takes over, it should not be mistaken for your true self.

Ultimately, becoming fully conscious of your Being is the key to developing strong, authentic relationships with others. While, as previously mentioned, men and women are only part of a whole, this fact will be immaterial if you are whole within yourself. You may feel the subtle tug of desire for completeness, but your inner body will be fully content. This is because you will no longer have a 'relationship with yourself', you will truly be yourself.

Being an 'outsider' in your group may indirectly help you get in touch with your Being. If you are dealing with homosexuality, for example, you may have already had to separate yourself from traditional ideas about who you are. Just take care not to let this aspect of yourself become your new identity.

CHAPTER 9 - The Truth About Happiness

According to Tolle, happiness and **inner peace** are two different things. Happiness depends on certain conditions being met. Inner peace is not dependent on any situation or condition. The key to inner peace is to understand that negative situations are only so because we view them that way, instead of viewing them as opportunities for enlightenment. This means understanding that, really, nothing is positive or negative—though, for the purposes of this book, it was easier to label some things that way. Truthfully, things just are as they are.

Take this understanding with you into difficult situations. When facing the death of a loved one, of course you will not feel happy, but you can feel at peace. This is a prime example of Being. For situations that you cannot do anything about, the key to peace is to **accept things as they are**. For situations, you can change, do what you can and then accept the results.

Most of the 'bad' things that come into your life are only labeled so due to unconsciousness. We constantly create our own drama by not allowing the present moment to simply be. There is still impermanence, there are still things that cause pain, but if you are enlightened, they can no longer affect you as they once did.

In life, everything moves in cycles. These are an essential part of your life. 'Down' cycles—times where you experience pain—are the most important. It is only through these experiences that we can connect to the spiritual realm. Even your physical energy moves in cycles. Just as 'down' cycles in experience are important for learning, so are 'down' cycles in energy. These times when you feel run down or are ill are a perfect opportunity for tuning into the Source for regeneration.

Another thing that will help is to remember that all things are impermanent, both positive and negative. This means that while you can accept the negative and embrace the joy, they no longer need to be a part of you. Eventually, they will all fade, but your true self will remain. You cannot achieve salvation by anything you do or acquire; your resistance to anything that is or will be is primarily futile. Any changes you make to counteract your experience will ultimately be temporary, just like the experience. Understanding this will put you at a turning point—after which, you choose either despair or enlightenment.

Primary examples of this acceptance of life can be found in nature. Observe plants and animals. They are masters of accepting what is without resistance. If they experience a conflict with one another, it is brief. Then life goes on as if nothing happened.

In previous chapters, Tolle discussed the importance of using negative emotions like sorrow and anger as signals to pay more attention to the moment. Another thing that you can practice to enhance this ability is a visualization technique. When you are experiencing a negative reaction, imagine yourself becoming transparent, then as mentioned before, look at the situation objectively, then let it go. Allow the negativity to simply pass through you.

If you find that, even through these exercises, you find you have still not reached those feelings of inner peace, this is probably because you are still approaching it as something you acquire. Remember it is not something that you should seek. It is simply something that you **do**. Think of yourself as a deep lake. The surface may become disturbed by outside elements, but within the depths, all is still.

This feeling of awareness will help you to become more compassionate to others. Think about it: if you are fully acknowledging that you are a vessel of the Source, as are all living things, then you are all connected. That means you can no longer say "I have nothing in common with this person." In reality, you are both living life as manifestations of the Source.

One powerful visualization that can help you with this is often called 'die before you die'. This requires you to become fully aware of your physical body. Understand that even as of now, your body is slowly degrading. One day, it will crumble into dust and become part of the earth. Accept this and remember that while your physical form dies, it is not who you are. Your Being will live on.

Tolle believes that the body and death are ultimately an illusion, since your consciousness never dies. Your body exists because you believe in death. Your true nature is concealed within your physical body. In order to access it, you must accept that your body is the tool you need to reach it. That is why your primary task is not to create a better world, but to reach a new state of consciousness where you understand that this world is an illusion. Embodying this state is what will enlighten others.

Some may feel called to alleviate the suffering of the world. This is where it is important to understand that all evils are the result of unconsciousness. So, you cannot eliminate them until you eliminate unconsciousness. Focus not on the outer suffering, but the inner enlightenment.

This will help you make change—not by fighting unconsciousness, but by raising awareness of the present moment.

CHAPTER 10 - The Definition of Surrender

Some readers may wonder about Tolle's instance on 'surrender'. They may be concerned that if we do not feel the need for change, nothing will ever get done. Tolle clarifies that surrender does not mean passively putting up with any situation. For the purposes of this book, it simply means to 'yield' rather than to actively oppose. And this is only on your innermost level. You can still permit your outer body to actively oppose, but your inner body should remain tranquil and accepting. Otherwise, your emotions will be what drives your actions, rather than your connection to the Source.

At this point, you may still wonder where your motivation for action comes from if non-judgement is your Source perspective. On the contrary: Tolle believes that this will help you see more clearly what needs to be done. By focusing on the present moment—on one task at a time—and focusing on what you can do now, instead of worrying about the future. Many of our problems arise or are made worse by our resistance to them, rather than simply dealing with things as they are.

Surrender also does not mean being cut off from our feelings. Instead, it means that we should accept our feelings as they are, but not let them rule our decisions. Allow yourself to feel the feeling. Keep your focus on that emotion—not on the person or situation that you think caused it. Giving that feeling your full attention is the essence of surrender.

People have done this in the past unintentionally. Many people feel that they have 'found God' through periods of suffering. This is because, through their pain, they have been forced to connect with the Source.

As you move toward enlightenment, you may become especially concerned for people who seem to 'choose' pain. Remember that choice requires consciousness, which they do not have. They are simply identifying themselves through their pain, just as you have done in your own way. This is often done through previous experiences that have conditioned them to associate abuse with love or something similar.

You will know that you have truly surrendered when you no longer need to ask if you have or not.

CONCLUSION

Ultimately, Tolle believes that time and death are illusions—for beyond all this, our consciousness lives eternal. The pain and suffering we feel on a daily basis should not be allowed to control us. The key to true salvation and inner peace is to immerse ourselves in the present. If we cease to dwell on the past or fear for the future, we will soon discover the enlightenment found within the present moment.

In addition, when we cease to identify ourselves with our pain, our emotions, or our thoughts—we can then begin to understand that who we truly are is beyond all of that. Who we truly are is an extension of one another and an extension of the Source. Once we achieve this enlightenment, we will no longer feel the need to complete ourselves with physical habits, relationships, or possessions. Our inner selves will be completely at peace, knowing we alone are enough.

RICH REFRESH

Chapter 1: The Definitions of Being

- Being is the eternal life beyond the mundane; it is the indestructible essence of every living thing. Ultimate enlightenment can be found when we embrace this Being instead of restricting ourselves to our external selves.

- Our continuous, unconscious thoughts are our greatest obstacle toward enlightened awareness. To overcome this, we should take the time to listen to our inner dialogue and our emotions—but with an objective demeanor. We must not equate our identity with our thoughts or emotions; this is called 'ego'. You can also quiet this dialogue by turning your focus to the present moment.

- Negative emotions stem from your loss of awareness of who you are. Alternatively, positive thoughts (love, peace, and joy) are connected to your state of Being. Pleasure is not categorized as positive because it relies on something outside of yourself.

Chapter 2: The Trouble With Pain

- The majority of human pain is unnecessary; we often cause it ourselves by failing to accept the present. When we focus too much on the future or dwell too much on the past, we ignore the precious nature of the present moment.

- Pain manifests as negative emotions and actions, such as abuse, violence, and mental illness. It is important to pay attention to your own emotional reactions in an objective way. Giving these reactions biased attention will only fuel their power. Then, turn your focus to the present.

- Fear is not essential to our survival; it is triggered by excessive focus on the past or future. Instead of allowing our fears to rule our actions, we should view the present in an objective manner, using our past experiences to help us determine our approach. This strategy will help us avoid unnecessary conflict and suffering.

Chapter 3: The Truth About Suffering

- You do not need to understand the inner workings of your mind to achieve enlightenment. Your mind is not your identity. The key to your enlightenment is to accept your mind for what it is: a tool for your true self.

- Time is an illusion. The only truth is the present moment. In your practice of living in the present, you will learn better from your past and set goals for your future in a much healthier way—because you will keep your focus on the actions you can take now, rather than later.

- Problems are also illusions. We must view these issues as situations—things we can change, or things we must accept. Dwelling on them emotionally without taking action will only bring us pain.

Chapter 4: The Problems of the Past

- As your perspective changes, what you experience will too. Work to improve your perception of the present. Then, when you must work within the confines of time for practicality's sake, your attitude will be more productive toward the situation and it will be easier for you to return to your state of inner peace when you are finished.

- Practice living in the moment at all times, even in simple situations. Ask yourself: "Am I at ease at this moment? Why or why not? This practice of consciousness will not only help your day-to-day life, but also help you deal with more complicated issues.

- Do not ignore negative emotions. They act as a signal that your perspective must change and/or that action should be taken. When you do choose to take action, work to do it from an objective place.

Chapter 5: The Potential in the Present

- To help yourself live in the moment, you must control your thoughts by maintaining your sense of self-awareness. One way that you can do this is by asking yourself: "What is my next thought going to be?" If you are in a state of presence, it may take time for your next clear thought to arrive. Take advantage of this silence. This will help you know what it feels like to be in the Now. Soon, you will be able to lengthen these moments of freedom from your unconscious thoughts.

- The Presence is your mostly-unconscious connection to your divine self—your connection to the Source. Christ (the eternal consciousness of Jesus) is the awakened version of this connection. Tolle believes that the second coming of Christ is actually this enlightenment in all of humanity. When we seek to connect with our Being, we are actually connecting with ourselves as an extension of Christ—a divine vessel of the Source.

- Everything in existence has Being. You are a thread in the weaving of all existence. Your Being is eternal, and is connected to everything around you. Your vessel may change and die, but your Being lives forever.

Chapter 6: Connecting the Dots

- Your Being is your true self, free from the restrictions of body, mind, and pain. Be aware of this life force within your body. The more often you do this, the easier it will become. One way to do this is to meditate, bringing your focus to each part of your body in turn and maintaining awareness of the different feelings that arise.

- The body is not something to be ignored or judged. It is an important tool for reaching enlightenment. We must work to be aware of our body and accept it for what it is. This will help us overcome pain and suffering and allow us to connect with our Being. It will also help improve physical health, slowing the process of aging and fighting disease.

- All spiritual teachings are derived from a single source. There is one master that manifests in various forms. Since we are all connected, we too are a part of that Source power.

Chapter 7: The Source and Death

- If you are having difficulty becoming aware of your inner body, some things that can help are: eliminating external distractions, sitting in a position that keeps

73

your spine straight and your body alert, and bringing your focus to your breath whenever you get distracted. Ultimately, practice will help you improve.

- There are two parts of your body: the outer body (physical) and the inner body (spiritual). Your inner body is a portal to the Source—connecting with it will help connect you to Christ. Other portals include: the present moment, silence, and space.

- Love is not a portal to Christ. Instead, love is a by-product of your connection. Death, however, is a portal. It is your last chance to access the Source. At this moment, accepting the source will bring your Being into a state of eternal consciousness, while rejecting it will cause you remain unconscious until you start all over again in another physical body.

Chapter 8: The Truth About Salvation

-   We cannot rely on our relationships to give us salvation. The feelings we get from romantic love are temporary. Salvation can only be found in the Now. We cannot wait for a moment in time to save us, since time is an illusion. If we develop a strong connection to our Being, we can prevent many of the problems many relationships have.

-   Salvation gives us freedom from fear, suffering, and our feelings of incompleteness. By living in the Now, we live with God and we achieve that salvation. God is the one life that connects us all.

-   Each relationship is an opportunity for unconscious issues to come to light. Remaining aware of these issues and maintaining your spiritual practice will help you to achieve enlightenment.

Chapter 9: The Truth About Happiness

- Happiness and inner peace are not the same thing. Happiness depends on the situation around you. Inner peace exists despite your current experience. Painful experiences are great opportunities for practice; accept that this moment is what it is and turn to the Source for regeneration.

- All of our experiences are impermanent. Eventually all of that will fade and only your Being will remain. This is why you cannot achieve salvation by anything you acquire or do. You can only reach it by connecting with the Source.

- If you are still having difficulty experiencing these feelings of inner peace, remember that it is not something that you should seek. It is something that you should simply do. You are a deep lake: ruffled by the world outside, but calm and peaceful within.

Chapter 10: The Definition of Surrender

- No matter what action you take, let your connection to the Source drive your actions. Maintain your sense of inner peace as you make your way in the world. Accept your feelings as they are, but do not let them rule your decisions.

- Surrender means to yield to the present moment. Focus on what you can do right now, rather than worrying about the past or future. You will know that you have truly surrendered when you no longer need to wonder whether you have or not.

- People who seem to choose pain do not have the consciousness to do otherwise. They are making their pain their identity. This is something you must remember not to do. You are not your emotions, thoughts, or suffering. Your true self is your Being—your connection to the

Source. It is your job to be the example of enlightenment for these people.

Last but not least, remember to visit us at www.summareads.com because we have some really special bonus for you!

This is SummaReads Media, your **#1 learning partner**, signing off right now and we look forward to speaking to you again in another one of our books! Bye for now!

CPSIA information can be obtained
at www.ICGtesting.com
Printed in the USA
BVHW040954210220
572990BV00009B/803